I0441427

Links between Communication Competency and Social Competency during and after an Artist's Career

Impact and Ramifications over Time for the Artist

SHAHAB NAHVI

abbott press®

A DIVISION OF WRITER'S DIGEST

Abbott Press books may be ordered through booksellers or by contacting:

Abbott Press
1663 Liberty Drive
Bloomington, IN 47403
www.abbottpress.com
Phone: 1-866-697-5310

ISBN: 978-1-4582-1405-8 (sc)
ISBN: 978-1-4582-1406-5 (e)

Library of Congress Control Number: 2014902268

Printed in the United States of America.

Abbott Press rev. date: 2/27/2014

To my wife, Sara, with love and affection

Contents

Abstract

An examination of artists and their lifestyle, particularly how their propensity to fully immerse themselves in their art creates isolation and disconnectedness that over time leads to a long-term impact on their social and communication skills and the ability to communicate and relate with non-artists and other artists, assisted by stereotype reinforcement. In addition to the author's firsthand experience as an artist, research articles discussing social and communication competency and film documentaries on artists are incorporated, and the Vaganova Ballet Academy and Kirov Ballet Company are used as a case study. In the conclusion, recommendations for how artists can retrain themselves to develop their social and communication skills are provided.

Keywords: communication competency, social competency, artists, non-artists, language, communication deprivation, isolation, stereotyping, retraining, dancers, musicians.

Introduction

In his documentary, painter Gerhard Richter declared: "Talking about painting is not only difficult, but perhaps pointless too, you can only express in words what words are capable of expressing, what language can communicate. Painting has nothing to do with that" (Kufus & Belz, 2011). Bernard Taper describes Choreographer George Balanchine's behavior outside the world of dance as "diffident" (1963, p. 231), meaning lacking self-confidence in communication.

> He had, his whole life long, an almost
> physical aversion to writing, so that he would
> telephone long distance almost anywhere
> rather than write a letter and, when pressed to
> write, would invent improbable and ingenious
> reasons for avoiding it. He didn't even care to
> read letters if he could help it. (p. 176)

Although there have been studies on creativity and what makes a creative person, there has been no critical examination of the artist's life and the possible impact it has on their social, communication, reasoning or cognitive abilities.

The goal of this paper is not to disrespect artists but to emphasize and highlight communication difficulties they may experience living among non-artists (regular people). It is conceivable that artists themselves are unaware of the issue, as if two different cultures are trying to communicate with one another. However, this does not mean that there are no difficulties among artists themselves. As a former classical dancer who has observed artists in different forms of art and has experienced this shared difficulty, I write in hopes that former and current artists who read this paper will know that they are not alone and that others do experience it as well, to varying degrees. I will question why certain utterances are common among dancers and artists, such as that they "felt naïve," "unsure," or "shy," or "couldn't get the words out," and "couldn't explain [myself]." Examples will also be given of what worked for me and others to improve our communication skills. The first step to resolving a problem is as always to acknowledge its existence.

Method

Laurie A. Meamber (2000, p. 44) in her article, "Artist Becomes/Becoming Artistic: The Artist as Producer-Consumer," suggests that artists internalize their art ("artist becomes"), so that their life and art become one, and "becoming artistic" results in life becoming infused with art so tightly, the life experience itself is being artistic, leading to being and creating without effort. When outsiders, non-artists, look at art and artists and examine them, they report something similar to this. It is mysterious. When one reads about zen and zen masters from the Far East, the implication is the same. It is in fact what zen masters have been pointing out: Creating without effort the zen way. However, in Eastern philosophy the zen master, after mastering an instrument, puts it aside and extends his experience to his life and, therefore, his life becomes his art. Meamber cannot make this connection since in the West (a consumption world) one has to have a product to sell, to be consumed; "Artists are thus both producers and consumers of art" (p. 44). Therefore, my intention is to look at art from the inside out, from the point of view of an artist in the West.

Representative sample

Although classical dancers are frequently mentioned in this article, classical musicians and other artists could easily be substituted. A sample of artists in various fields was used to demonstrate shared communication and social competency experiences. For general gender references, masculine and feminine pronouns were alternated throughout the paper and, thus, should be viewed as interchangeable.

Materials and Procedure

Many of the articles referenced are studies by psychologists on social and communication competency, comprehension and a lack thereof, and the impact of these on adolescents. Documentaries were chosen without concern for their particular subjects. The intention was to find out with what frequency the dialogue revolved around communication and how effective the artist's communication was as far as the artist was concerned. We will also look at stereotypes and their impact on the artist's life. An artist timetable for the Kirov Ballet Company and its associate school will be provided as an example of how much time is required to master the art and maintain high quality performance.

Communication competency

Visual picture

Imagine an individual grabbing a rope hanging from a tree and using it to swing towards the river and drop into the water. If he is apt and has the physical ability, whether by daily exercise or physical work, he will hold himself up on the rope until it is time to let it go and drop into the water, and he will have a sense of satisfaction in completing his task. However, if he is not prepared and does not know his own limits, he will find himself at the end of the rope before it's time and at the side of the river, on the rocks.

Well, communication is similar in that it requires daily practice to be efficient, and since today's life mostly revolves around communication (receiving and sending, written and verbal, between friends and family and/or on a job), it will depend on it. When dancers or artists who mostly rely on non-verbal communication begin to master the skills required to perform their tasks, it means that they have invested years of their lives in training and performing in non-verbal communication. Therefore, their communication skills will not be up-to-par, which is most evident when transitioning to a new career due to injury, age, or prolonged period of training with little or no job prospects. Depending on what level they had reached in their artistic careers, they will very often have to make do by securing jobs outside of their artistic training.

Generally, these individuals do not realize they lack necessary skills since they assume that if they speak the language used in the country they live in, when they stop performing they will be able to find something else to do without any difficulty. However, they soon find that is not the case and that they lack even the ability to explain what they mean or want. Hence, they find they have to retrain. For example, former New York City Ballet principal dancer, Suzanne Farrell, commented in the documentary *Never Stand Still:* "I had to learn how to speak. I could no longer speak with my movement. I had to retrain myself in a way of being understood" (Penman & Honsa, 2011). This comment has been made by many dancers but this realization is enhanced when the non-verbal type of communication has been eliminated. It is like a sighted man losing his sight or perhaps the other way around. The above is supported by a nine-month study by Meamber (2000): "Many of the artists interviewed here struggled… to liberate or expand the notion of what is art, who they are as artists" (p. 45).

Communication deprivation

Barnett, Gustafsson, Deng, Mills-Koonce, and Cox (2012, p. 376) in their article "Bidirectional Associations Among Sensitive Parenting, Language Development, and Social Competence" state, "Language is a social tool that develops through interaction with others, and the ability to use language provides opportunities to gain social skills." What happens when an artist deprives herself eight hours a day or more, and for decades, from using social and communication skills? Choreographer Pierre Lacotte in the documentary *Ballerina* compared a dancer's life to "joining a convent in terms of self-deprivation" (Podetti, Brolli, & Gentot, 2009). Similarly, Richter argued that: "Each painting is an assertion that tolerates no company" (Kufus & Belz, 2011). In life, when we deprive ourselves of food in order to stay thin for the sake of a career or appearance, there is a price to pay. When we deprive ourselves of communication and society for many years, again for the sake of a career, what would be the price?

Social competency as it relates to communication competency

Social media

To answer the above question, let us look at the problem from a different angle. What would happen if our society became obsessed with a way of communicating that did not require face-to-face communication? What would be the impact of such a change on communication and social skills?

Social media in fact illustrates just that. It is a device through which as one communicates, the more time spent on it, the better the performance. One can easily shift through material without worrying about hurting anyone's feelings. The main purpose of this form of communication is to expedite communication and remove the need for face-to-face dialogue, which mimics what artists have been doing to themselves throughout their careers. The drawbacks of social media are discussed in "Death of Small Talk Britain" (Mccann, 2013). Removing oneself from engaging in face-to-face communication ultimately results in a feeling of discomfort when one does have to do so. The more the discomfort intensifies, the less anyone wants to engage in face-to-face communication, which will affect social skills over time. Barnett et al. (2012, p. 376) suggest that poor social competence could lead to poor language skills, or "over time, limited language abilities may lead to fewer social interactions and opportunities to gain social competence." Along the same lines, the British study on social media found that more than half of the individuals studied felt they were not as strong as they should be at talking with people. The increased usage of these devices is recent, and even though standard communication was used (written words), and not abstract (movement, musical notes), social skills were affected. Artists who become obsessed with their instruments communicate using an abstract language and during the course of a day have limited face-to-face communication with others. When they use verbal language it is for an immediate need and does not require learning new vocabulary. Given the importance of social and communication skills, it should not come as a surprise that artists are often described as eccentric.

Effect of lack of communication and social competency over time

Having stated that poor social skills could lead to poor language skills, which ultimately affects individuals of elementary to high school age, very often dancers who are training to become professionals have no choice but to abandon traditional schooling and attend lower quality classes to achieve a high school education through a GED program. This is due to years of depriving themselves of social interaction and its chances for communication, which leads to poor language skills, simulating a second language speaker in many ways. Mancilla-Martinez and Lesaux (2011, p. 1545) in "The Gap Between Spanish Speakers' Word Reading and Word Knowledge: A Longitudinal Study" argued, "Given that oral language skills play an increasingly important role over time in reading comprehension achievement, students must not only obtain adequate word reading skills, but their oral language skills must also continue to develop (Paris, 2005; Snow & Kim 2007)."

Concentrating all of one's effort on developing a subject for several years can put a crimp in social and verbal abilities, if that subject does not require them. To what degree depends on the original abilities or disabilities of the individual. One could say that development creates change. It is good to develop mastery of an instrument, but not when one loses the ability to communicate with others in exchange.

Feeling disconnected

If you consider that "oral language skill starts developing in infancy and continues to develop throughout life," and that it is the "critical foundation for reading, writing, and spelling…the 'engine' of learning and talking" (National Institute for Literacy, 2009), what happens to your communication skills if a career like dancing comes along when you are ten years old, and it does not necessarily rely on them? What would happen if you did not use your language skills often? Would you feel disconnected and unable to communicate your thoughts?

Because dancers and other artists do not engage in social activity early on, many of them have a truncated experience, which reduces their sense of competence, self-determination, and shared understanding of their society and culture. Shared values (which are part of belonging to a group or country) facilitate identity development in its narrowest form, particularly the artist culture, its vocabulary and language. "In the homonomous [*sic*] [Homonymous] tendency the person seeks to fit himself into larger organizations…the social group, a meaningful world order, etc. Characteristic examples of the trend toward homonomy [*sic*] [Homonymy] are social, religious, ethical and esthetic attitudes" (Angyal, 1941 as cited in Roe, 1946, p. 6). And, while solitary activity "provides an opportunity for self-reflection, contributing to identity development" (Fenech, 2008, p. 295), much of which dancers and other artists do throughout their career, at the same time it diminishes the opportunity to socialize and invariably vocalize one's views. In the case of Wolfgang Amadeus Mozart, according to Wallace Brockway and Herbert Weinstock (1958), sense of competence and self-determination, that is the ability to make decisions, was lacking.

> Until his twenty-fifth year it never entered
> his head to question, much less to disobey,
> Leopold Mozart's fiats on every subject
> under the sun, and he never tired of saying
> that he considered his father 'next to God.'
> Unfortunately, this touching attitude was
> partly an excuse for his own unwillingness
> and inability to make decisions for himself.
> It had served a certain purpose in the past,
> but was no weapon for the struggles for the
> future. (p. 134)

Feeling a need to recreate

The purpose and outcome of verbal or written communication is to be understood, yet to what extent the communicator is able to do so largely depends on his experience and the amount of effort made not only to understand his subject but also himself. However, no matter how prepared he may be, he cannot change the condition of the recipient's ability to listen, analyze, understand, and report what he has heard. Much of that depends on the recipient's skills. Communication competency requires not only an ability to state one's mind, but also to receive and listen to other people's ideas. If one area is weak, the other will be too. And this may be one of the main reasons why artists constantly look for new methods to communicate at a level of production not required from any other human endeavor, and is most intensely felt in the West because of the need to produce with respect to the culture of consumption. If you are not producing, you are not relevant. The rate of exchange is inadequate considering what artists have to give up, not only with respect to the ability to socialize and communicate with others, but artistically as well. Most often they have no share in what their company produces even though the company exists only because its members participate in its creation and the creation of the art. Here it is important to recall a landmark ruling:

> U.S. District Judge, Miriam Goldman Cedarbaum held that from 1956 to her death in 1991, [Martha] Graham was an employee of the [Martha Graham] center and that works created by her during that period constituted work-for-hire and thus belonged to her employers. Cedarbaum ruled that earlier works had been assigned by Graham to the center after its creation. (Segal, 2002)

That is, no matter how important the choreographer may be to the company, she is still an employee. This becomes very important when discussing stereotypes.

To explain it another way, if you have not spoken a language with some regularity for say 10-20 years, you will find that you are rusty and that the words and sentences do not come to you easily to explain yourself. Nor should you expect that your listening ability and comprehension will be at its best. Dancing or performing a particular instrument intensely will have the same effect, where after 10-20 years your communication skills will be diminished in what is considered the realm of regular people. If you have a sibling who did not participate in the performing arts, all other things being equal, he will be more apt to deal with the real world. This effect and experience is long term across social, psychological, and physical planes. The individual will appear withdrawn, shy, unsure, overwhelmed, and naïve, constantly looking for ways to express themselves.

Fear of negative evaluation and shyness

In *Pina*, a documentary about modern dance choreographer Pina Bausch, one of her dancers commented:

> Meeting Pina was like finding a language finally. Before I did not know how to talk and then she suddenly gave me a way to express myself. A vocabulary. When I began, I was pretty shy. I still am. And, after many months of rehearsing she called me and said, 'You just have to get crazy.' And, that was just the only comment in 20 years. (Ringel, Ossard, Bolzli, & Wenders, 2011)

This example demonstrates that not only highly skilled classical dancers but also modern dancers experience a lack of ability to communicate, and the level of communication that exists among them regardless of culture and language. Competency issues in social and communication skills lead to shyness, which is a result of "fear of negative evaluation" (Coplan & Weeks, 2009, p. 245). This in turn causes the individual to "lag behind" in communicative skills because of a "less frequent rate of engagement in social interactions (Coplan & Armer, 2005)" (as cited in Coplan & Weeks, p. 248). The terms shy and awkward were used by Brockway and Weinstock (1958) to describe classical musicians such as Ludwig van Beethoven ("… [a] rather uncouth man, with his painful awkwardness and social tactlessness…", p. 175); Franz Peter Schubert ("…shy and awkward", p. 255); and Robert Schumann ("…shy [and] taciturn…", p. 304), among others.

Naivety

Social skills in a relationship can be difficult because of the unpredictability of emotional reaction. The individual, not having enough practice despite his age, added to the lack of abundant experience in cognition and reasoning, which leads to certain choices, projects the appearance of naivety. In a conversation, she might come across a word such as "empathy." She might not know what it means, or she does but does not know what to do with it due to lack of experience. To provide an analogy, in music you may come across the term "piano" (soft volume). How do you play softly? Does it mean not loud? How you accomplish it depends on the instruction you received initially, when learning the instrument. With dancing, the teacher may say "pointe" as the late Stanley Williams did in his class. If you are not familiar with it, you may think he's referring to pointing your foot, which in part he is; however, the term "pointe" in his class and at the New York City Ballet was all-encompassing, which included being on time with the music. So, if an individual has not had the opportunity to use a word such as empathy, or even just use it often enough, knowing what it means will not achieve a proper response. "Empathy is not simply a matter of trying to imagine what others are going through, but having the will to muster enough courage to do something about it. In a way, empathy is predicated upon hope" (West, 1999, p. 12).

Due to the absence of life experience, compounded by a lack of word knowledge and its application, the artist will be socially inept, psychologically stressed, and physically tired because what she has to endure is outside the realm of her art form. What she used to do for many years was habitual. In the real world, every step must be thought out and analyzed especially if there is no family support or government assistance to help with the transition. This is particularly true in the U.S. where art is consumed and artists are considered transitory.

Communication and social competency expectations on artists

The term transitory leads us back to "outsiders" versus "insiders". Most studies of artists are written by non-artists who refer to artists as "outsiders". However, the same term is used by dancers to identify non-dancers/artists. As Meamber (2000) stated, "Although they [dancers/artists] are removed from the world, they are not distant from its effect and are able to reflect, react, and comment upon it" (p. 44). How can this statement be true? How can a dancer comment and reflect on his society when he is so far removed from it as to require retraining of his language? The general belief is that artists reflect and comment on society because art has to have a grander agenda to exist in a consumer-driven society, which cannot see art being produced for the sake of art itself. If there is any reflection or comment by the artist, most often it is accidental, happening when the life of the artist crosses paths with an issue that troubles the society. Society in fact burdens the artist to be its conscience. This is not the true role of the artist. In the documentary *Never Stand Still*, Choreographer Paul Taylor discusses his piece *De Suenos*: "It is supposed to be like a dream. You can't quite make sense of the logic behind it. But, people will try, you know. And, uh, I wish them luck" (Penman & Honsa, 2011). Art is similar to clouds in the sky. The viewer sees what he wants to see. Maybe even what he needs to see. But, this is not an artist's doing. When Richter was asked, "What were you thinking of [when you were painting]?" he replied, "You can't think of anything. Painting is another form of thinking" (Kufus & Belz, 2011).

Role of stereotypes as a form of communication and means of maintaining status quo

When Meamber (2000) states that "[dancers/artists] are removed from the world," it follows the idea that they are separate from other people and, therefore, their creativity is mysterious and beyond the grasp of non-artists (regular people). "Artist and Nonartist: A Comparative Study" by Bernice Eiduson (1958) identified problems such as this with respect to other researchers of her time:

> Even more unfortunate is the fact that these studies have unwittingly served to reinforce some of the previous stereotypes about artists that they are persons apart from other persons, that their very separateness and uniqueness are in some way essential ingredients for their productivity and for the contributions that they make…whose disturbance has to be considered, accepted, and praised because presumably it forms the basis of his creativeness. (p. 13)

A stereotype is formed to remember and understand a story for the sole purpose of sharing (communicating) with ease (Lyons & Kashima, 2006, p. 68). This suggests that if you want to be remembered by others, you do what the stereotype requires. Then, stereotyping and exploitation can go hand-in-hand. Stereotypes give people what they expect. In some circumstances, it can be a method of control. Quite often it is the stereotype that attracts new artists. It is the stereotypes that permeate movies involving classical dancers, musicians, and other artists. The artists are never seen being pensive, jotting down notes or reading, and very often are shown skipping class or not being studious. The question that never arises is how they learn the details of their trade, such as reading music or choreographing classical stories, mythologies and fables, all of which requires a deep understanding of the material.

Once a stereotype is established, movies such as *Turning Point* have little difficulty in finding an audience, as the audience knows what to expect. It is this stereotype that sets the stage for control over dancers who have come to believe that an "artist" is a "person apart from other persons...whose disturbance has to be considered, accepted, and praised because presumably it forms the basis of his creativeness" (Eiduson, 1958). In Choreographer George Balanchine's case, contrary to his biographer Taper (1963, p. 65), who points to technique being more important to Balanchine than inspiration when it came to creating, his actions spoke volumes to his students and subordinates in formatting the stereotype. Edward Villella and others came to believe that when Balanchine fell in love with one of his students, creative juices flowed.

> There was always a ballerina who inspired him. He'd fall in love with her and then usually marry her. I was fascinated. So was everyone else. I had the feeling all the ballet mothers sitting in the hall would have gladly thrown their twelve-year-old daughters at him on the chance he'd become entranced with one of them and make her a star. (Villella, 1992, p. 25)

Therefore, stereotype gave Balanchine power through the belief held by his subordinates. The combination of non-verbal communication and a limited storyline is enough to keep dancers in check considering what has been described above regarding their behavior and understanding of the world.

A stereotype weakens in light of additional information. Maria Tallchief in the 2005 documentary *Ballets Russes* stated:

> And I have written in my diary how nice he [Balanchine] is to me…and this and that, and you know and it wasn't much after that, we were up in San Francisco or something…and he asked me to marry him. I said, 'George, I

don't love you.' And he said, 'But that doesn't
make any difference. Love will come one day'.
(Goldfine & Geller)

Tallchief at the time was 19 years old, and Balanchine was
42, when they wed in 1946. Their marriage was annulled in
1952, as a few years earlier, according to Villella, Balanchine
had a relationship with another student of his, Tanaquil
LeClercq, who was at the time 17 years old (but had joined
his school at age 11 in an audition where Balanchine was
chief judge (Taper, 1963, p. 220)). "He was oblivious of
everyone but her. By then everyone knew he was in love
with her. He was casting her in many new roles and wanted
to marry her" (Villella, 1992, p. 25). This pattern continued
throughout his career. Taper commented, "Always a dancer
under his aegis, always young, not yet fully formed, either as
person or dancer" (p. 228). Balanchine's requiring students
to participate in this stereotype, and the acceptance of it
by those around him, his knowledge that a young dancer
who is naïve, shy, unsure and has limited life experience is
unable to say no, his confidence strengthened by knowledge
that her career is in his hands, demonstrates the power of
this stereotype, which has already been adopted by future
generations.

What helps to break down a stereotype like this one is an
understanding that artists are not "persons apart from other
persons" (Eiduson, 1958), and that the choreographer or
director is an employee of the company. (As stated above,

the court ruled that Martha Graham was an employee of the Center.) A stereotype will strengthen as inconsistent portions of the story are omitted ("stereotype inconsistent"). However, full disclosure of the history will weaken the stereotype as more people come to accept it (Lyons & Kashima, 2006, p. 59).

Time constraints hindering investment in developing social and verbal skills: Vaganova Ballet Academy and the Kirov Ballet Company as case study

Here it is necessary to provide an example of the training required of an art medium to demonstrate the amount of time needed to master the art. Whereas in the West hope and faith are the pathways to choosing a particular art, often with little or no rigorous examination, and it is this hope and faith, directed by "listen to your heart," that drives the business of the performing arts and makes it profitable, the Kirov Ballet Company and its associated school are different.

Vaganova Ballet Academy takes children at age ten. Of the hundreds of girls who apply every year, 30 or so are admitted. Only half of them will complete their study. Prior to admission, many of them have received training elsewhere. Within eight years of entry, their training is over. That means, the school takes only 240 students in eight years and produces 120 graduates during the same period of time.

Of this group, one female each year is accepted to the Kirov Ballet Company. In short, they make a very concentrated effort to choose dancers with the most potential for the eight years they are going to invest in. At the same time they eliminate a large sum of the population who apply and therefore do not deprive them of social experiences since they ultimately will not succeed. The school is also not motivated by monetary gain to increase student volume. The Kirov Ballet at any given time has 120 female dancers and 100 male dancers. "At school, you are busy during the day, whereas in the theater you are on stage every night. It is an entirely different experience," said Ludmila Safronova, teacher at Vaganova Ballet Academy (Podetti et al., 2009).

The schedule for the Kirov Ballet is as follows. "At 10:40 a. m. it's classical dance class until mid-day, rehearsals comes right after that, then they have a break, then they prepare for the show at 6 or 7 p. m., putting on makeup, and finish at 11 o'clock at night. The next day the same," said Corps de ballet member Evguenya Obraztsova (Podetti et al., 2009). Again, this leaves little room for developing social and verbal communication skills. The above circumstances also apply to other dance companies and artists. If you are starting at ten years of age and your career ends at say 30 or 40, what happens if you become severely injured? Or your years of training do not lead to a substantial career? Will you have enough social and verbal skills to make a living elsewhere?

Conclusion and recommendations for how to retrain

Artists deprive themselves of face-to-face communication for prolonged periods of time for the sole purpose of immersing themselves in their art. In so doing, social and communication difficulties arise. They may appear as shy and naïve due to an absence of life experience. This article describes a correlation between poor social competency and poor language competency, and contends that an artist's so-called separateness is generated because of it. In some instances, these deficiencies are a means to use and abuse artists, assisted by stereotype reinforcement. It is essential to recognize these weaknesses and find ways to improve them to change the quality of life for artists.

Retrain

- Find activities that are meaningful to you. Moving forward will require a goal that has sufficient information to motivate and challenge without creating a problem of overload, which could lead to shutting down.

- Intentionally develop oral language skills by understanding what words mean and the connections among them, and the social rules of conversation (take turns).

- Read books, and practice conversation and listening to be able to better explain how you feel.

- Use abstract vocabulary (take college courses).

- Try to have a deeper understanding of the words you have heard and how they make you feel. Check the dictionary for in-depth understanding of a word. Find a reason to talk.

- Consider leisure activity, as it "reinforce[s] social/cultural roles and values [and] facilitate[s] social approval and self identity, through feedback from others" (Fenech, 2008, p. 295). The feedback element is a major component of an artist's life. However, for dancers, musicians and artists, understanding leisure activity, let alone engaging in it, could be a difficult concept.

References

Barnett, M.A., Gustafsson, H., Deng, M., Mills-Koonce, W. R., & Cox, M. (2012). Bidirectional associations among sensitive parenting, language development, and social competence. *Infant and Child Development, 2*, 374-393.

Brockway, W. & Weinstock, H. (1958). *Men of music* (Rev. ed.). New York: Simon and Schuster.

Coplan, R. J. & Weeks, M. (2009). Shy and soft-spoken: Shyness, pragmatic language, and socioemotional adjustment in early childhood. *Infant and Child Development, 18,* 238-254.

Eiduson, B. T. (1958). Artist and nonartist: A comparative study. *Journal of Personality, 26,* 13-28.

Fenech, A. (2008). The benefits and barriers to leisure occupations [Guest editorial]. *NeuroRehabilitation, 23,* 295–297.

Goldfine, D. (Producer), & Geller, D., Goldfine, D., Hawk, R., Turnbaugh, D.B. (Directors). (2005). *Ballets Russes* [Motion picture]. New York, NY: Zietgeist Films.

Kufus, T. (Producer), & Belz, C. (Director). (2011). *Gerhard Richter painting* [Motion picture]. Germany: Zero One Film and Terz Film.

Lyons, A., & Kashima, Y. (2006). Maintaining stereotypes in communication: Investigating memory biases and coherence-seeking in storytelling. *Asian Journal of Social Psychology 9,* 59–71.

Mancilla-Martinez, J., & Lesaux, N.K. (2011, September/ October). The gap between Spanish speakers' word reading and word knowledge: A longitudinal study. *Child Development 82*(5), 1544-1560.

Mccann, J. (2013, May 30). Death of small talk Britain: 'We have become obsessed with social media and haven't spoken to a stranger for more than six months'. *Daily Mail.* Retrieved August 8, 2013, from http://www.dailymail.co.uk/news/article-2333298/ Britons-obsessed-social-media-havent-spoken-stranger-months.html

Meamber, L.A. (2000). Artist becomes/becoming artistic: The artist as producer-consumer. *Advances in Consumer Research 27,* 44-49.

National Institute for Literacy. (2009). *Learning to talk and listen: An oral language resource for early childhood caregivers.* [Brochure]. Washington, D.C.: Author.

Penman, N. (Producer) & Honsa, R. (Director). (2011). *Never Stand Still* [Motion picture]. New York, NY: Moving Pictures.

Podetti, F., Brolli, Y. (Producers), & Gentot, L. (Director). (2009). *Ballerina* [Motion picture]. New York, NY: First Run Features.

Ringel, G., Ossard, C., Bolzli, C. (Producers), & Wenders, W. (Director). (2011). *Pina* [Motion picture]. Berlin and Paris: Neue Road Movies and Eurowide.

Roe, A. (1946). Artists and their work. *Journal of Personality 15*, 1-40.

Segal, L. (2002, August 24). Martha Graham Dance Center wins custody battle. *Los Angeles Times*, p. A13.

Taper, B. (1963). *Balanchine.* New York: Harper and Row.

Villella, E. (1992). *Prodigal Son.* New York: Simon and Schuster.

West, C. (1999). The moral obligations of living in a democratic society. In David Batstone & Eduardo Mendieta (Eds.), *The Good Citizen* (pp. 5–12). New York: Routledge.